Bootloader Source Code for ATMega328P using STK500
For Debian Linux
Including Makefile and Test Program

First Edition

Herb Norbom

Author of:
Robot Wireless Control Made Simple with Python and C
Python Version 2.6 Introduction using IDLE
Python Version 2.7 Introduction using IDLE
Python Version 3.2 Introduction using IDLE and PythonWin
Bootloader Source code for ATMega168 using STK500 for Microsoft Windows
Bootloader Source Code for ATMega168 using STK500 For Debian Linux
Bootloader Source Code for ATMega328P using STK500 For Microsoft Windows

Where we are aware of a trademark that name has been printed with a Capital Letter.

Great care has been taken to provide accurate information, by both the author and the publisher, no expressed or implied warranty of any kind is given. No liability is assumed for any damages in connection with any information provided.

Table of Contents

PREFACE

A large part of this project is on how to configure and load programs on to an ATMega328P microchip. I am going into some depth on the 'BOOTLOADER'. The complete source code for the bootloader.c, testAVRlib.c and uart.c is included. The 'Makefile' for each program is included. For our bootloader we need to have a device to load that software, I will be using an STK500. This project is aimed at readers running Debian-Linux, although other versions of Linux generally apply.

In this project we will start with a microchip that does not have a bootloader or bootstrap on it. We will spend some time looking at and burning the fuses and lock bits for the ATMega328P. We will be writing a bootloader program for the chip. We will build a library for our common function. We will progress to writing our application test program code and loading it on to the microchip. One of my goals is to give you the knowledge to become as independent as possible from suppliers. I will be using open source or otherwise free software. We will be using Atmel microchip's and when possible Atmel software. As a point of reference I am currently running Debian Release 6.0.7 (squeeze) on an old PC with an Intel(R) Pentium(R) 4 CPU 2.40GHz. The Kernel Linux is 2.6.32-5-686. I am also using the GNOME Desktop 2.30.2. I will be using the bash shell.

PROCESS STEPS

- Of course you need the hardware, chips, ISP device, misc. parts, etc.

- You need the software for the programs avr-libc, avrdude, gcc-avr, avrdude-doc, and binutils-avr.

- You need to setup your directories.

- Build your breadboards for programing the chip (We will build two).

- You need to burn the fuses and lock bits

- You need to write and load your bootloader.c program, including writing the Makefile.

- Build a library for storing the UART common files.

- We will write a small test program to test your bootloader, you will write another Makefile for loading the test program to your microchip.

Supplies And Devices

Unless you have programed microchips before you are going to need some devices and some parts. Our chips do not have a bootloader installed. To set the fuses on the chips you are going to need a chip programmer or In-System-Programer(ISP). We are going to be working with the Atmel chip called the ATMega328P. The following list gives you a complete parts list and you can substitute as you like.

Part	Possible Source	Source Part #	Min Qty	Approx. Price	Ext. Price
ATMega328P-PU	Mouser Electronics	556-ATMega328P-PU	1	2.24	2.24
Linear Regulator-5V	Mouser Electronics	511-L7805CV	2	0.59	1.18
Crystal 14.7456	Mouser Electronics	695-HC49US-147-U	2	0.52	1.04
Capacitor 104 0.1uF	Electronix Express	14DK050.01U	2	0.10	0.20
Capacitor approx 220uf 35V	Electronix Express	14ER035220U	2	0.15	0.30
Resistor Kit –for selection	Electronix Express	13RK7305	1	11.95	11.95

Part	Possible Source	Source Part #	Min Qty	Approx. Price	Ext. Price
Half-Size Bread Board	AdaFruit	ID:64	2	5.00	10.00
Hook Up Wire 22AWG solid core	get best price	you do not need a lot			
Breadboard-friendly SPDT Slide Switch	AdaFruit	ID: 805	1	1.95	1.95
USB to TTL Serial Cable	AdaFruit	ID: 954	1	9.95	9.95
AVR STK500 USB ISP Programmer	Sure Electronics	RDB-DA11114	1	22.99	22.99
LED	Mouser Electronics (buy several)	749-5AC BUT there are many to choose from	1	0.30	0.30
ZIF socket 28-pin(optional)	AdaFruit	ID: 382	1	3.00	3.00

For the resistors and capacitors, this project requires only a couple of each. If you are buying from Electronix Express consider the kits, as there is a minimum order limit of $20.00. If you want to burn fuses and load a boot-loader you need a device similar to the STK500. There are many of them on the market. For all of the items listed this is a possible parts and POSSIBLE supplier list. For the low priced items you may want to buy several as multiple shipments will end up costing more. While I have used these suppliers I am not saying they are the best or the least expensive. I am not affiliated with any of them.

Linux – C Library

This software will give you the libraries needed for compiling your C programs. You will want the AVR 8-bit Toolchain that is appropriate for your computer. You can also check Synaptic Package Manager, aptitude and apt-get as possible sources. You can do a quick search, use 'avr' as the query. You are going to need at a minimum 'avr-libc, avrdude, and gcc-avr'. You should plan on getting the documentation for avrdude, 'avrdude-doc'. I installed using the following commands:

- apt-get install avrdude
- apt-get install gcc-avr
- apt-get install avr-libc

Executable for avrdude and gcc-avr were installed in /usr/bin. Under /usr/lib/avr an extensive directory tree was built that we will refer to later. You need to get the software installed before continuing.

Testing Avrdude

There are a number of methods for running 'avrdude', we are going to use the 'Terminal Prompt' I will refer to it as just a 'prompt'. Open a prompt and type 'avrdude' this should give you a list of valid avrdude commands. If it does not then something is not installed correctly. There are a number of possible explanations, the simplest being that you somehow did not install in your PATH. You may need to precede avrdude with 'sudo'.

Work Directories

We are going to be writing a number of programs and it can get very confusing where they are located. Also from a backup view point it is nice to have them in a separate directory, probably several. I suggest you make a separate directory now. I called my directory 'HerbKit328'. Within HerbKit328 you are going to need some sub-directories. I suggest the following, which we will go into more detail as we progress.

- compileLinkBootloader328 For our bootloader.c program and its Makefile

- uploadBootloader328   Script files for chip fuse setting and bootloader program Makefile for installation of bootloader
- herbClib328   Uart program, header for our application programs and Makefile
- testAVRlibrary328   Test program to make sure all is working and Makefile

Text Editor

You are going to need a text editor for working with the various files. I will be using 'Geany', see the appendix for information on it. You can also use Vim or Vi or any other text editor you are comfortable with.

Script File

Note what directory your prompt opens in. You will probably want to create a script file to take you to your work directory. Our first directory will be one for keeping our fuse and lock settings used to configure the microchip. I will call my directory 'uploadBootloader328'.

The script file I made is shown in the following. (I will mark the beginning and end of files with START** and END** statements, do not include in your files. Remember to give the script execute privileges. Enter chmod u+x stk500work328 on the command line. See the Appendix for a quick refresher. Under Linux running the script is okay once you understand that you need to start the script with a special command. You will just use a '.' one space in front of the script name. Like this '. stk500work328'.

```
START **
# stk500work328                 items after a # are a comment
#  Herb Norbom 8/27/2013
echo "hi there, I will be changing to a new directory"
cd Herbkit328/uploadBootloader328
ls -l
END**
```

The script should print out our cute message and change to the new directory and list the contents, which is probably empty at this point.

STK500 SETUP

If you are using a device similar to the STK500 your set up may be similar, but the following description is for the STK500 purchased from Sure Electronics. The first item is to build out our breadboard. Take your time. I have set my board up to have the microchip's pin 1 in position 1 on the breadboard. This works great for the left side, but doesn't help with the right side as you can see in the diagram. Hopefully you are familiar with the breadboard, but if not you will quickly figure out that the left and right half of the board are not connected, unless you connect them. If you look at the breadboard rows 26 and 27 you see the connections between the positive and negative rails. I am using an outside power source to the breadboard, required by my STK500. I connect the positive power source to the 5V voltage regulator input and the voltage regulator output to the positive rail of the breadboard. The outside power source can be a 9V battery, or in my case an AC/DC converter with 9V DC output. In any event your microchip needs 5V DC.

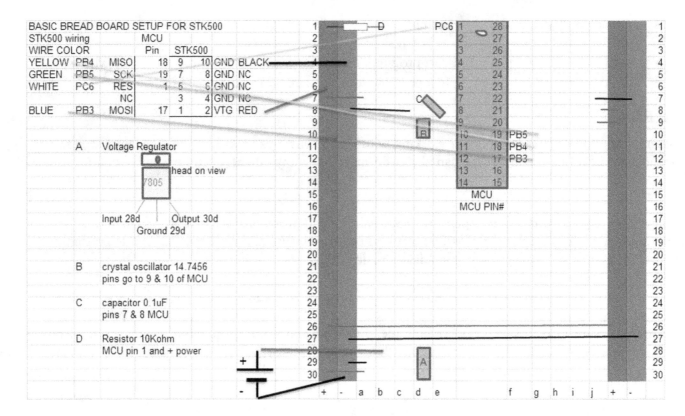

One of the confusing items of the STK500 is in connecting the flat or ribbon wire strip to the pig tail. Remember on a flat or ribbon strip the red wire is for pin 1. Also I am sure you remember that on a connector there is usually some type of indicator as to which pin is 1. On my setup, very hard to see in the picture there is a little arrow shape on both the connectors, that also indicates pin 1, so match them up.

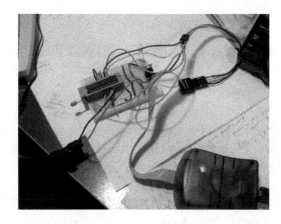

The picture shows an LED, this is optional. I just put it on to remind me when the auxiliary power is on. If you add the LED make sure you also add a resistor. As I found the wiring from the STD500 through the ribbon or flat cable to the 10 pin connector, then to the 6pin connector, then to the breadboard a little confusing I prepared the following exhibit. I hope it helps.

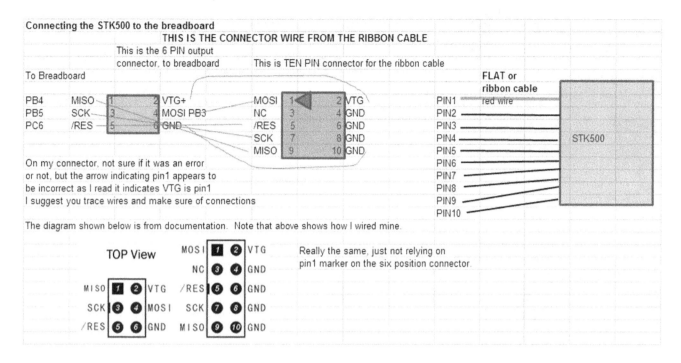

Testing Our STK500

You will be plugging the USB cable into your computer. I always have the power off and the USB connector unplugged when I am inserting or removing a chip. Remember static electricity is not your friend, so ground yourself. You may also also need to add external power to your breadboard.

Chip in place, USB connected and with external power on. Get to your command prompt execute your script to get to your work directory, my script stk500work does it. Type the following on the command line, we are just going to try to read the chip, no writing at this point.

```
sudo avrdude -c stk500 -p m328p -P /dev/ttyUSB0 -b 115200 -v
```

You should get something very similar to the following, which I broke into several screen shots. You may want to try leaving the baud rate out of your commands. I have found this to generally work also. But you are relying on system wide avrdude.conf settings, I think it is better to enter the baud and know what speed you are running at. If you are having trouble connecting see the Appendix for what I hope is help.

```
sudo avrdude -c stk500 -p m328p -P /dev/ttyUSB0 -v
```

```
┌─────────────────────────────────────────────────────────────────────────────┐
│ ▣            herbnorbom@debian: ~/HerbKit328/uploadBootloader328      _ □ x    │
├─────────────────────────────────────────────────────────────────────────────┤
│  File  Edit  View  Terminal  Help                                             │
│ herbnorbom@debian:~/HerbKit328/uploadBootloader328$ sudo avrdude -c stk500 -p m3 ▲│
│ 28p -P /dev/ttyUSB0 -b 115200 -v                                              │
│ [sudo] password for herbnorbom:                                               │
│                                                                               │
│ avrdude: Version 5.10, compiled on Jun 27 2010 at 00:21:42                    │
│          Copyright (c) 2000-2005 Brian Dean, http://www.bdmicro.com/          │
│          Copyright (c) 2007-2009 Joerg Wunsch                                 │
│                                                                               │
│          System wide configuration file is "/etc/avrdude.conf"                │
│          User configuration file is "/root/.avrduderc"                        │
│          User configuration file does not exist or is not a regular file, skippi│
│ ng                                                                            │
│                                                                               │
│          Using Port                      : /dev/ttyUSB0                       │
│          Using Programmer                : stk500                             │
│          Overriding Baud Rate            : 115200                             │
│          AVR Part                        : ATMEGA328P                         │
│          Chip Erase delay                : 9000 us                            │
│          PAGEL                           : PD7                                │
│          BS2                             : PC2                                │
│          RESET disposition               : dedicated                         │
│          RETRY pulse                     : SCK                                │
│          serial program mode             : yes                               │
│          parallel program mode           : yes                               │
│          Timeout                         : 200                               │
│          StabDelay                       : 100                               │
│          CmdexeDelay                     : 25                                │
│          SyncLoops                       : 32                                │
│          ByteDelay                       : 0                                  │
│          PollIndex                       : 3                                  │
│          PollValue                       : 0x53                              │
│          Memory Detail                   :                                    │
│                                                                             ▼ │
└─────────────────────────────────────────────────────────────────────────────┘
```

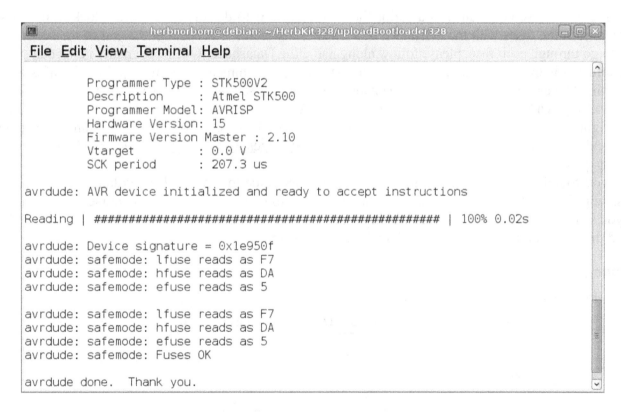

File Edit View Terminal Help

				Block	Poll		Page				
Polled											
Memory Type	Mode	Delay	Size	Indx	Paged	Size	Size	#Pages	MinW	Max	
W ReadBack											
-----------	----	-----	-----	----	------	------	----	------	-----	---	
-- ---------											
eeprom	65	5	4	0	no	1024	4	0	3600	36	
00 0xff 0xff											
flash	65	6	128	0	yes	32768	128	256	4500	45	
00 0xff 0xff											
lfuse	0	0	0	0	no	1	0	0	4500	45	
00 0x00 0x00											
hfuse	0	0	0	0	no	1	0	0	4500	45	
00 0x00 0x00											
efuse	0	0	0	0	no	1	0	0	4500	45	
00 0x00 0x00											
lock	0	0	0	0	no	1	0	0	4500	45	
00 0x00 0x00											
calibration	0	0	0	0	no	1	0	0	0		
0 0x00 0x00											
signature	0	0	0	0	no	3	0	0	0		
0 0x00 0x00											

File Edit View Terminal Help

```
         Programmer Type : STK500V2
         Description     : Atmel STK500
         Programmer Model: AVRISP
         Hardware Version: 15
         Firmware Version Master : 2.10
         Vtarget         : 0.0 V
         SCK period      : 207.3 us

avrdude: AVR device initialized and ready to accept instructions

Reading | ################################################# | 100% 0.02s

avrdude: Device signature = 0x1e950f
avrdude: safemode: lfuse reads as F7
avrdude: safemode: hfuse reads as DA
avrdude: safemode: efuse reads as 5

avrdude: safemode: lfuse reads as F7
avrdude: safemode: hfuse reads as DA
avrdude: safemode: efuse reads as 5
avrdude: safemode: Fuses OK

avrdude done.  Thank you.
```

The above setting were not for a new 'raw' chip but from one I have programed previously. The key elements we are looking for at this stage are the fuse settings and the Device Signature. Before we get to far into this you need to recognize that the values shown for lfuse, hfuse, and efuse are hex values. I suggest you check on the web and find a site for converting hex to decimal. I am going to prepare a table that breaks down the fuses into their individual bit names. I will also show what the settings are for a new 'raw' chip and for what setting I want for my chip. Review the Datasheet for the ATMega328P under Boot Loader Support to check what I am suggesting. The important point is that the Device Signature we use in our program and Makefile must agree with the microchip's signature. The ATMega328P has a Device Signature of 0x1e950f as shown in the example. See page 298 of the Datasheet.

SETTING THE FUSES AND LOCK

Other than potentially destroying your chip this section is relatively straight forward. Be careful, double check your work and verify the instructions I give you with the Datasheet. If you purchased chips that have the boot-loader installed you may be able to skip this section. If you haven't been looking at the Datasheet now is the time, get familiar, page references are to the Datasheet. We will be configuring our chips to include the following items:
- Use 1,024 words for size of Boot Loader Section
- Preserve EEPROM memory through Chip Erase
- Set Brown Out level MinV=2.5V
- Divide clock by 8
- Full Swing Crystal Oscillator (see page 30, section 8.4)
- Do not allow SPM to write to the Boot Loader Section.

Be sure you are working with an ATMega328P that has the Device Signature 0x1e950f, see page 298.

You can put the fuse commands in a script file and execute it to do all the fuses and lock at one pass. I generally burn the fuses with the assistance of a Makefile, which I will detail at the end of the section. I am going to go through each fuse, please follow along using the Datasheet. One of the many items that you may find confusing is that the value of '1' means the byte is unprogrammed. One more point of confusion deals with setting that are 'not used'. The documentation says that the setting is a '1'. You will notice on a new chip that the setting is a '0'. If you try to set a 'not used' Byte to a '1' chances are it will not be accepted. I am sure you are going to have more questions about avrdude. The documentation on my machine is installed at usr\share\doc\avrdude.doc. Also available on line http://packages.debian.org/squeeze/avrdude-doc

I hope you found a site to assist you in converting the hex value to binary. The avrdude display shows the fuse settings in hex, but to understand the setting you need to convert to binary. Of course when burning the fuse you will need to use a hex value. Writing fuses and lock bits are a complex subject and you need to be warned that you can fry or 'brick' your microchip, so be careful.

Extended Fuse Byte

Let's start with the 'EFuse', see page 296

	Extended Fuse Byte	Bit No	Default	Mouser	HerbKit	References
	not used	7	1	0	0	
	not used	6	1	0	0	
	not used	5	1	0	0	
	not used	4	1	0	0	
	not used	3	1	0	0	
BODLEVEL2	Brown-out detector	2	1	1	1	page 296, Table 27-6

BODLEVEL1	Brown-out detector	1	1	1	0	
BODLEVEL0	Brown-out detector	0	1	1	1	
	HEX VALUE		FF	7	5	

Let's read the Fuse values and get used to the avrdude commands and displays. Type the following command to display the current settings.
sudo avrdude -c STK500 -p m328p -P /dev/ttyUSB0 -b 115200 -v

To burn the efuse the command is:
sudo avrdude -c STK500 -p m328p -P /dev/ttyUSB0 -b 115200 -U efuse:w:0x5:m
Run the display command and make sure that the fuse value changed.

High Fuse Byte

'HFuse', see page 297

	Fuse HIGH Byte	Bit No	Default	Mouser	HerbKit	References
RSTDISBL	External Reset Disable	7	1	1	1	
DWEN	debug WIRE enable	6	1	1	1	
SPIEN	Enable Serial Program and Data Downloading	5	0	0	0	not accessible in serial programming
WDTON	Watchdog timer Always On	4	1	1	1	see page 50
EESAVE	EEPROM memory is preserved through the Chip Erase	3	1	1	0	want to preserve EEPROM memory
BOOTSZ1	Boot Size	2	0	0	0	page 291, Table 26-13
BOOTSZ0	Boot Size	1	0	0	1	
BOOTRST	Reset Vector	0	1	1	0	page 281, Table 26-4
	HEX VALUE		D9	D9	D2	

To burn the hfuse the command is:
sudo avrdude -c STK500 -p m328p -P /dev/ttyUSB0 -b 115200 -U hfuse:w:0xd2:m

Run the display command and make sure that the fuse value changed.
sudo avrdude -c STK500 -p m328p -P /dev/ttyUSB0 -b 115200 -v

Low Fuse Byte

'LFuse', see page 298 Table 27-9

	Fuse LOW Byte	Bit No	Default	Mouser	HerbKit	References
CKDIV8	Divide clock by 8	7	0	0	1	we want to divide by 8
CKOUT	clock output	6	1	1	1	not using
SUT1	Select start-up time	5	1	1	1	Table 8-8 page 32
SUT0	Select start-up time	4	0	0	1	Table 8-8 page 32
CKSEL3	Select Clock Source	3	0	0	0	Table 8-9 page 32

CKSEL2	Select Clock Source	2	0	0	1
CKSEL1	Select Clock Source	1	1	1	1
CKSEL0	Select Clock Source	0	0	0	1
	HEX VALUE		62	62	F7

To burn the lfuse the command is:
sudo avrdude -c STK500 -p m328p -P /dev/ttyUSB0 -b 115200 -U lfuse:w:0xf7:m
Run the display command and make sure that the fuse value changed.
sudo avrdude -c STK500 -p m328p -P /dev/ttyUSB0 -b 115200 -v

Lock Bit Byte

'Lock Bit Byte', see page 294 Section 27.1 **Remember '1' means unprogrammed**

	Fuse LOW Byte	Bit No	Default	Mouser	HerbKit	References
	not used	7	1	0	0	
	not used	6	1	0	0	
BLB12	Boot Lock bit	5	1	1	1	see page294,table 27-1
BLB11	Boot Lock bit	4	1	1	0	see page294,table 27-1
BLB02	Boot Lock bit	3	1	1	1	see page294,table 27-1
BLB01	Boot Lock bit	2	1	1	1	see page294,table 27-1
LB2	Lock Bit	1	1	1	1	see page294,table 27-2
LB1	Lock Bit	0	1	1	1	see page294,table 27-2
	HEX VALUE		FF	3F	2F	
	Based on above BLB0	MODE	1	1	1	see page295,table27-3
	Based on above BLB1	MODE	1	1	2	see page295,table27-3

Page 295 Table 27-3

BLB0 MODE=1	No restrictions for SPM or LPM accessing the Application section.
BLB1 MODE=1	No restrictions for SPM or LPM accessing the Boot Loader section.
BLB1 MODE=2	SPM is not allowed to write to the Boot Loader section.

The lock bits are just a little bit more complicated to view. We will write them to a text file and view them with our text editor. We want to look at the current settings prior to making any changes. The command for this is:
        sudo avrdude -c STK500 -p m328p -P /dev/ttyUSB0 -b 115200 -U
lock:r:HerbKit328/uploadBootloader328/fuse_lock:h
(Note the above command is one line, but if you want to continue a command on a new line enter a backslash and you will see a > displayed for you to continue your command.)

We are writing the fuse settings to a file named 'fuse_lock' in our current directory. You need the whole path from your Home directory or it will just put the file in your Home directory. You can use any name you like for the file. As a side note you can use the same technique to write the fuse settings to individual files.

Take a look at the permissions for the file we just created by typing 'ls -l' and you will most likely see that root is the owner of the file. To change this to be the owner you are running as type the following. 'chown herbnorbom fuse_lock' (of course use your user name). Type ls -l again and see if the owner changed.

To burn the lock bits the command is:
sudo avrdude -c STK500 -p m328p -P /dev/ttyUSB0 -b 115200 -U lock:w:0x2f:m

To check, run the command to write the lock settings to the file, make sure that the lock settings changed.

Script file to burn FUSES

I like to have a script file for writing the fuse settings. I have two files as I have sometimes had trouble setting the lock and fuses in one file. Later on I will give you my Makefile which has all the commands for the fuses, lock and installation of our application program. I saved the script file in the 'uploadBootlloader328' directory the first script file is named 'STK500write328Fuses'. Remember to give the script execute privileges. Under Linux running the script is okay once you understand that you need to start the script with a special command. You will just use a '.' one space in front of the script name.

  Like this   '. STK500write328Fuses'.

START**

```
# display setting fuses
avrdude -c STK500 -p m328p -P /dev/ttyUSB0 -b 115200 -v
#  should get Device Signature=  0x1e950f
# EFUSE
avrdude -c STK500 -p m328p -P /dev/ttyUSB0 -b 115200 -U efuse:w:0x5:m
# HFUSE
avrdude -c STK500 -p m328p -P /dev/ttyUSB0 -b 115200 -U hfuse:w:0xd2:m
# LFUSE
avrdude -c STK500 -p m328p -P /dev/ttyUSB0 -b 115200 -U lfuse:w:0xf7:m
```

END**

Script file to burn LOCK BYTES

Make a separate script file for the writing the lock byte hex value. You can look at the output displayed to verify the new setting or run command to write the 'fuse_lock' setting to the file. I saved the script file in the 'uploadBootlloader328' directory the script file is named 'STK500write328lock'. Remember to give the script execute privileges. To run use a '.' one space in front of the script name. Like this '. STK500write328lock'.

START**

```
# write LOCK BYTES ATMega328P using STK500

avrdude -c STK500 -p m328p -P /dev/ttyUSB0 -b 115200 -U lock:w:0x2f:m

#  should get Device Signature=  0x1e950f
```

END**

BOOTLOADER

Our microchip needs to have a 'bootstrap' or 'bootloader'. Before getting into the bootloader it may help you to understand the concept, think of it as just another program. We will write ours in 'C'. In the very simplest terms this is a program that the microchip executes as it starts or 'boots' and instructs the program to run the application or load a new program. While this program is just another program it does have some specific abilities as it needs to set up the hardware. This program needs to be placed in a specific section or position within the microchip's memory called the Boot Loader Section or 'BLS'. The BLS resides in the flash memory. I hope you see in the Datasheet that the flash memory is or can be divided into two sections, the BLS and Application sections. This is a complex subject and you need to be warned that you can fry or 'brick' your microchip, so be careful.

BOOTLOADER PROGRAM

Now that you are somewhat comfortable with the STK500 and avrdude we will move into the meat of the book. We are going to write a bootloader program using avr-gcc and the 'C' programming language. A reference starting point is http://nongnu.org/avr-libc/user-manual/ . If you downloaded the documentation you may find it in usr/share/doc/avr-libc.

You may have found the various bootloader examples out on the web to be very complex and generally missing a key piece of the pie. There are a number of free bootloader.hex files available on the web. But, if you are here you are like me, and want to know how it works.

We are going to write a bootloader.c program that is specific for the ATMega328P and the ISP STK500. To keep this solution as simple as possible, we are writing code for one chip and one ISP. I have used standard header files, no auxiliary configuration or header files. While the program will use UART, I have included that start-up or 'init' settings in the program to avoid having another level of confusion.

At this point I would hope that you have a general working knowledge of the "C" programing language, and a handle on the text editor, I will be using Geany. I am going to provide some discussion first and then the complete program source code. Within the source code I have added comments to assist us in understanding what we are trying to do. Leave the comments out or modify as you like.

I suggest that you open your program editor and type the following comments to get a program started. Remember in "C" comments begin with a // or you can do the block comments. For this book I am marking the start and end of the program with START** and END**. Don't include the markers with your code.

START**

```
//Bootloader for ATMega328P uses AVR109 and AVR910 protocols
//Herb at RyMax, Inc. 8/31/2013
//this program will always run first, decision made based on PB0(high or low)
//on loading new program or running application
```

END**

Save your program with the name bootloader.c, in the directory 'compileLinkBootloader328' or whatever directory you want to designate.

Include Headers

Next we need to talk a little about the header files we want our program to include. As I said we are going to use that standard header files that are included with avr. It is worthwhile to know where they are, you can open them with your editor. I strongly advise that you DO NOT CHANGE any of them, just look if you like. The files are located on my computer at: usr/lib/avr/include/avr. These files save you a tremendous amount of work. The first one we are going to include is <avr/io.h>. By including this header file you begin the definition of our microchip. This file gives us access to our specific microchip, which we will later define in our Makefile as 'ATMega328P' or m328p using the avrdude commands.(Much more on that latter). We are going to need the following headers, some defines, some work variables and the section where the 'code' is written. Add the following to the end of your program, and save the program. (At the end of the section are screen shots of the entire bootloader.c program.)

START**

```
// the includes are in usr/lib/avr/include/avr
#include <avr/io.h>   //includes sfr_defs, portpins, common, version
//above also selects iom328p.h
//portpins defines the PORTs, direction, pins, registers, etc.
#include <avr/boot.h>//turns off interrupts, SPM Control, Fuse bits, & more
#include <avr/eeprom.h>
#include <avr/pgmspace.h>
#include <util/delay.h>
//see Atmel .com/images/doc2568.pdf for information on AVR910
#define _AVR910_DEVCODE 0x35
uint16_t flash_loc ;    // flash use byte address
uint16_t eeprom_loc;   // eeprom use byte address
uint16_t temp_loc;           //temp holder
//use the noinline attribute to save bytes
//use static to reduce size, see AVR4027,doc8453.pdf
#define noinline __attribute__((noinline))
int main(void){
//we are going to be entering code here, make sure you do not lose the '} 'at the end as we add code.
}
```

END**

We now have enough of a program to write our Makefile and test the very basics. Generally there are a number of assigns done in the Makefile. For example, setting a variable name for baud rate, and assigning the baud rate to the variable at the beginning of the file. We are going to make this a very specific Makefile and try to avoid the variables. As we are learning I think this is easier. The goal for this Makefile is to compile our bootloader.c program, link the program as needed, produce an object file and a hex file. We are going to include some list files just to help you get familiar with them but they will not be needed for our steps here. Our Makefile will include the start position for the BOOT LOADER SECTION as defined by our fuse settings. While our bootloader.c program is just getting started I want to develop a complete Makefile for the purposes described above. The actual uploading of our hex program file will be covered later.

Makefile-compile

Open your text editor, and create a new file. Your filename will be 'Makefile' and you will save the file in the same directory as your bootloader.c program. Some general notes on Makefiles are appropriate. A comment is made with a '#' sign, this only applies to the beginning of the line. In our commands that we want to continue on a new line, end the line to be continued with a '\' backslash. While you can have multiple Makefiles in a directory you must be careful of the names and your actual command to start the Make process is slightly different. To keep our programs and actions separate and somewhat simple we will only have one Makefile per directory. There is some documentation in usr/share/doc/make. For additional information try http://www.gnu.org/software/make/manual/make.html .

I am going to list the entire Makefile for compiling, linking and generating support files in the following. I have included descriptions that you should not enter in your Makefile.

	DESCRIPTIONS DO NOT INCLUDE IN Makefile
# Makefile for bootloader	The # means this is a comment line.
all: compile	What we are processing with the make file. If just make is typed on command line will do all sections. If we type 'make compile', will just do that one section
compile:	Section defined.
avr-gcc\ -g\	We are using the avr-gcc compilier, -g for producing debugging information. Note the '\' means the command continued on next line.
-Os\	Optimize for size.
-mmcu=atmega328\	Specify the ATMEL AVR defined
-DF_CPU=14745600\	Two things, the '-D' defines a name, also setting the clock speed
-std=gnu99\	Set the language standard, we are using gnu
-DBOOT_SECTION_START=0x7800\	Two things, the '-D' defines a name, also giving hex value for start of boot section
-Werror\	Make all warnings into errors
-Wl,--section-start=.text=0X7800\	Linking, Wl (note this is a small letter L, not a '1'). Passing the item after the comma to the linker.
-o bootloader.o bootloader.c	Produce an output file named bootloader.o
avr-objcopy -j .text -O ihex bootloader.o bootloader.hex	Copy the bootloader.o file to the bootloader.hex file and use the library to change to the desired format
avr-objcopy -j .text -O ihex bootloader.hex bootloader.lss	Copy the bootloader.o file to the bootloader.lss file and use the library to change to the desired format
avr-objdump -S bootloader.o > bootloader.lst	Displays information about the bootloader.o in the bootloader.lst file.
@echo "*********"	Simple echo to print the stars
@echo "compiled for: atmega328"	Simple echo saying what is in the " "
@echo -n "bootloader size is: "	Simple echo saying what is in the " ", note it starts with -n which generates a new line.
@echo	Simple echo to print a blank line
@avr-size bootloader.hex	Displays size stats of hex file, uses the default format.
@echo "*********"	Simple echo to print the stars

You can have other sections than the 'compile:' included in your Makefile. Some people like to add a 'clean:' section to remove files, pursue other sections as you like. In a later Makefile we will have some additional sections.

BOOT_SECTION_START

I hope that the descriptions with the Makefile are adequate, but I know we need to talk some more about the start of the BOOT_SECTION_START. This can be confusing. First remember how we defined our fuses. We defined a boot section size of 1,024. Look back at the EFuse and the Datasheet page 291, Table 26-13. It is important to note that the 1,024 is words and not bytes. Our ATMega328P uses two bytes for every word. So our boot size is 2,048 bytes. The chip memory is organized with the Boot Section at the top of the flash memory. Our total flash memory is 32,768 bytes. The Datasheet, page 291, shows that for our 1,024 Boot Size, the Start-Boot-Loader-Section is 0x3C00. That hex value in decimal is 15,360. Now remember we are talking about 'words', to convert the 15,360 words to bytes we multiply by two and get 30,720 bytes. With our flash section ending at 32,768 bytes and the boot-section at the top of the flash section to get the start position we subtract 2,048 bytes from our total bytes of 32,768. This gives us a byte boot start of 30,720, which checks with our previously calculated boot start section. Of course, not quite done as we need to give the start position in hex format. So we convert the 30,720 bytes to hex and get 0x7800. If you play with the Datasheet and the memory definitions I think it all will fall into place.

Some other facts that may help are from page299, Table 27.5 with some math added.

WORD -bytes	PAGE-words	PAGE-bytes	No. of pages	FLASH size -bytes
2	64	128	256	32,768
given	given	2 x 64 = 128	given	64 x 256 x 2 =32,768

First Compile of bootloader.c

Open a prompt and change to the 'compileLinkBootloader328 directory. This directory needs to have our bootloader.c program and our Makefile. Type 'make' and press return. If all is well this will be your display. Notice that all the commands are displayed.

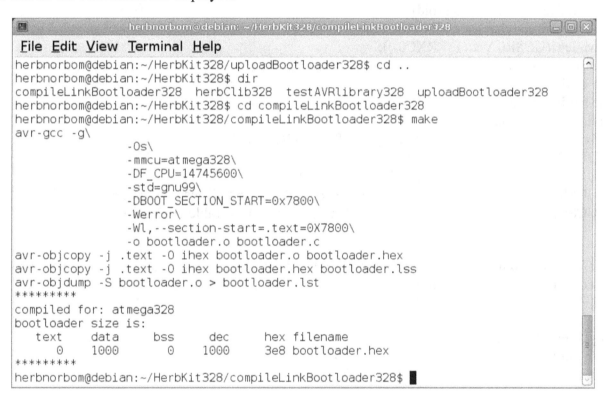

```
herbnorbom@debian: ~/HerbKit328/compileLinkBootloader328

File  Edit  View  Terminal  Help
herbnorbom@debian:~/HerbKit328/uploadBootloader328$ cd ..
herbnorbom@debian:~/HerbKit328$ dir
compileLinkBootloader328  herbClib328  testAVRlibrary328  uploadBootloader328
herbnorbom@debian:~/HerbKit328$ cd compileLinkBootloader328
herbnorbom@debian:~/HerbKit328/compileLinkBootloader328$ make
avr-gcc -g\
                -Os\
                -mmcu=atmega328\
                -DF_CPU=14745600\
                -std=gnu99\
                -DBOOT_SECTION_START=0x7800\
                -Werror\
                -Wl,--section-start=.text=0X7800\
                -o bootloader.o bootloader.c
avr-objcopy -j .text -O ihex bootloader.o bootloader.hex
avr-objcopy -j .text -O ihex bootloader.hex bootloader.lss
avr-objdump -S bootloader.o > bootloader.lst
*********
compiled for: atmega328
bootloader size is:
   text    data     bss     dec     hex filename
      0    1000       0    1000     3e8 bootloader.hex
*********
herbnorbom@debian:~/HerbKit328/compileLinkBootloader328$ 
```

After you successfully run this, look in your directory and you should see the additional files. You can use your text editor to view the bootloader.lss and bootloader.lst files. These files are about memory locations, mainly of use if you are having problems with your programs. (This is a screen shot after the entire program has been entered, your size at this point is only about 150 to 160.)

Bootloader – Communication Uart

In an attempt to keep this program as simple as possible we are putting the code for uart communication into our program rather than into separate header files. This section deals with putting characters and strings; getting characters; and defining our communication protocols. If you are following with the Datasheet look at the registers and you will get a feel for how the communication flow is controlled. For the protocols all that we need to set up in this program is the 'get' and 'put' functions, baud rate and the enabling of the transmit and receive procedures. Add this code just before the start of the 'int main(void) section.

START**

```
//output character
static noinline void uart_putc(uint8_t data)
        {   // loop until all data transmitted  see page 195
    while ((UCSR0A & (1<<UDRE0))==0);//if UDRE0=1 buffer empty & ready
    // put data in buffer
    UDR0 = data;}
//output string
static inline void uart_puts(uint8_t buffer[])
        {   // send until end of string
    while (*buffer != 0) {
        uart_putc(*buffer);
        buffer++;}}
//read character
static noinline uint8_t uart_getc(void)
        {   // wait for character to be received
        while (!(UCSR0A & (1<<RXC0)));
    /* return received byte */
    return UDR0;}
//init the hardware uart
static inline void init_uart(void)
        {   // set baud rate for 115,200 using F_CPU =14745600
        UBRR0H = 0;
        UBRR0L = 7;          //see page 202 set 115,200 baud
        UCSR0B = (1<<RXEN0)|(1<<TXEN0);//enable Receiver & Transmitter,pages 196-197
        UCSR0C = (1<<UCSZ01)|(1<<UCSZ00);} //page 197-198, Table 19-7, set for 8 bit
```

END**

After the 'int main(void) we need to add some variables and a call to our uart function. Add the following 3 lines of code, notice they are indented one tab stop.

START*

```
    uint8_t memory_type;
    uint16_t buffer_size;
    init_uart();
```

END**

In the code we just added we set up registers that turn on and off various features for USART, our serial protocol.   I have selected 115200 as our desired BAUD rate. This gives a very low error rate for the crystal oscillator we are using, and it is relatively fast. Our crystal frequency is 14.7456 MHz's.   Based on page 202, Table 19-11, we want to set the UBRRn register at 7. (We are using U2Xn =0, of the UCSRnA register that has an Initial Value of 0. See page 195 of Datasheet. We are not going to bother with setup of U2Xn, just know we are using it.)

After you have saved your program run the 'make' command again, after correcting any errors we will move on.

BOOT *Load New or Run Existing*

With our next section of code we want to be able to tell if our bootloader.c program should run a previously loaded application or if new application software is going to be loaded. With the ATMega328P pulling the PINB to ground, (using our switch or ground wire). Note, when we are ready to load our application program we will be using a different breadboard, described later. If pulled to ground we will want to load new application software if not pulled to ground we will run the existing application. We need to setup the PORT DATA REGISTERS for input and pullup. We also built in a delay to allow the chip registers setup to be completed. Add the following code after the 'init_uart(); statement. Use the same one tab indent.
START**

```
    DDRB &= ~(1<<PB0); //PORT DATA REGISTER set as input
    PORTB |= (1<<PB0); //PORT DATA REGISTER enable pullup
    // wait a little
    _delay_loop_1(200);//arbitrary number
```
END**

After you have saved your program run the 'make' command again, after correcting any errors we will move on.

Decision Time

In this section we will actually test the PINB and run sections of the code for either running the existing application or loading new application software. If PINB is pulled to ground with our switch we will go to the 'start_bootloader' section of code. If not pulled to ground we will jump to our application start address. Add the next section of code after the delayloop_1(200); statement, continue using the same one tab indent.

START**

```
  // bootloader test to see if new program to load
        if(PINB == 0) {//if PINB is pulled to ground
      goto start_bootloader;
    } else { //start application
      // see DataSheet page 68, jump to application program start of flash memory
      MCUCR = 0;
      asm("jmp 0000");}
start_bootloader:    // main communication loop with avrdude

    while (1)

    {   //these are commands from avrdude also look at AVR109 Protocol doc1644.pdf
```
//don't lose '}' at end of this section, should now have two of them at the end of your program.

```
        }
```
END**

After you have saved your program run the 'make' command again, after correcting any errors we will move on.

Communication with avrdude and STK500

This next section of code is the meat of the bootloader program. Here there is communication between our program and our soon to be created new Makefile for the uploading of the application program, not this bootloader program that we are working on now. In this section we will receive input from avrdude and respond accordingly. We will use the 'switch' and 'case' operations. I have tried to put comments in to help you find additional information. (At the end of this section I will show the entire completed program.) Enter the following code after the comment in the 'while (1) ' section. Don't lose the end of section markers '}'.

START**

```
    uint8_t avrdude_cmd = uart_getc();
    switch (avrdude_cmd){
      case 'P':  //Enter Programming Mode
            uart_putc('\r');
            break;
      case 'L':  //Leave Programming Mode
            uart_putc('\r');
            break;
      case 'a':  //Auto Increment Address
            uart_putc('Y');
            break;
      case 'A':  //Start address, we want to start at byte 0, but it
            //looks like avrdude needs us to read the address
            //so read and ignore
            temp_loc = (uart_getc() << 8) | uart_getc();
            eeprom_loc = 0;        //set to zero
            flash_loc = 0;         //set to zero
            uart_putc('\r');
            break;
      case 'e':  //Chip Erase, all pages in flash, as per lock-bits
            //bootloader section should be protected by lock-bits
            for (flash_loc = 0; flash_loc < BOOT_SECTION_START;
                  flash_loc += SPM_PAGESIZE) {
                  boot_page_erase_safe(flash_loc);}
            uart_putc('\r');
            break;
      case 'T':  // Select Device Type: received device type
            uart_getc();
            uart_putc('\r');
            break;
      case 's': // Read Signature Bytes: send the signature bytes for this MCU
            uart_putc(SIGNATURE_2);  //FROM iom328p.h  see Datasheet page 298 27.3
            uart_putc(SIGNATURE_1);
            uart_putc(SIGNATURE_0);
            break;
      case 't':  // Return Supported Device Codes, terminate with a nullbyte
            uart_putc(_AVR910_DEVCODE);
            uart_putc(0);
            break;
      case 'S':  // Return Software Identifier, send s[7]
            uart_puts((uint8_t *)"RyMax");
      case 'p':  // Return Programmer Type, 'S' for serial
            uart_putc('S');
            break;
```

```c
case 'E':   // Exit Bootloader
        uart_putc('\r');
        break;
case 'b':   // Check Block Support: return yes, another byte + block size
        uart_putc('Y');
        uart_putc(0);
        uart_putc(SPM_PAGESIZE);
        break;
case 'B':   // Start Block Flash Load, read buffer size (in bytes)
        buffer_size = (uart_getc() << 8) | uart_getc();
        // check buffer size not exceeded
        if (buffer_size > SPM_PAGESIZE) {
                uart_putc('?');
                break;}
        //read flash ('F') or eeprom ('E') memory type
        memory_type = uart_getc();
        if (memory_type == 'F'){
                uint16_t i;
                uint16_t temp_word_buffer;
                if (flash_loc > BOOT_SECTION_START) {
                        uart_putc(0);}
                uint16_t temp_address = flash_loc;
                boot_spm_busy_wait();
                // read data, wordwise, low byte first
                for (i = 0; i < buffer_size/2; i++) {
                        // get data word
                        temp_word_buffer = uart_getc() | (uart_getc() << 8);
                        // write data to temporary buffer
                        boot_page_fill(temp_address, temp_word_buffer);
                        // increment by two, since temp_address is a byte
                        // address, but we are writing words!
                        temp_address += 2;}
                // after filling the temp buffer, write the page
                boot_page_write_safe(flash_loc);
                boot_spm_busy_wait();
                // re-enable application flash section for read
                boot_rww_enable();
                // store next page's address, since auto-address-incrementing
                flash_loc = temp_address;
                uart_putc('\r');
        }
        else if (memory_type == 'E'){
            uint8_t temp_data;
            uint16_t i;
            for (i = 0; i < buffer_size; i++) {
                    temp_data = uart_getc();
                    eeprom_write_byte( (uint8_t *)eeprom_loc, temp_data);
                            eeprom_loc++;}
            uart_putc('\r');
```

```c
          }
         else {uart_putc('?');}
      break;
   case 'g':  // Start Block Flash Read, read byte counter
      buffer_size = (uart_getc() << 8) | uart_getc();
      // then, read memory type
      memory_type = uart_getc();
      // memory type is flash
      if (memory_type == 'F')
         {  // read buffer_size words
         uint16_t i;
         for (i = 0; i < buffer_size; i += 2) {
                 uint16_t temp_word_buffer;  //define 16 bit for word size
                 // read word
                 temp_word_buffer = pgm_read_word(flash_loc);
                 // send data as word
                 uart_putc(temp_word_buffer);              //low byte
                 uart_putc(temp_word_buffer>>8);           //high byte
                 // increment address by 2, since it's a byte address
                 flash_loc += 2;
      }}
      // if memory type is eeprom
      else if (memory_type == 'E'){
         uint16_t i;
         for (i = 0; i < buffer_size; i += 1) {
                 uint8_t temp_buffer;
                 // read and send byte
                 temp_buffer = eeprom_read_byte((uint8_t *)eeprom_loc);
                 uart_putc(temp_buffer);
                 eeprom_loc++;
      }}
      else {uart_putc('?');}
      break;
   default:   // default: respond with '?'
         uart_putc('?');
         break;
   }END**
```

Just as a point of clarification, at the end of the program you should have three '}'.

After you have saved your program run the 'make' command again, after correcting any errors we will move on. The complete bootloader.c source code follows, broken into sections for ease of displaying

BOOTLOADER.C source code

```
bootloader.c - /home/herbnorbom/HerbKit328/compileLinkBootloader328 - Geany

File  Edit  Search  View  Document  Project  Build  Tools  Help

Makefile × | bootloader.c ×

 1   //Bootloader for ATmega328p uses AVR109 and AVR910 protocols
 2   //Herb at RyMax, Inc. 9/1/2013
 3   //this program will always run first, decision made based on
 4   //PB0(high or low) for loading new program or running application
 5   // the includes are in dir usr/lib/avr/include/avr
 6   #include <avr/io.h> //includes sfr_defs, portpins, common, version
 7   //above also selects iom328p.h
 8   //portpins defines the PORTs, direction, pins, registers, etc.
 9   #include <avr/boot.h>//turn off interrupts,SPM Control,Fusebits,etc
10   #include <avr/eeprom.h>
11   #include <avr/pgmspace.h>
12   #include <util/delay.h>
13   //see Atmel .com/images/doc2568.pdf for information on AVR910
14   #define _AVR910_DEVCODE 0x35
15   uint16_t flash_loc =0;      // flash use byte address
16   uint16_t eeprom_loc =0;     // eeprom use byte address
17   uint16_t temp_loc=0;        //temp holder
18   //use the noinline attribute to save bytes
19   //use static to reduce size, see AVR4027,doc8453.pdf
20   #define noinline __attribute__((noinline))
21   //output character
22   static noinline void uart_putc(uint8_t data)
23      {   // loop until all data transmitted  see page 195
24      while ((UCSR0A & (1<<UDRE0))==0);//if UDRE0=1 buffer empty
25      // and ready put data in buffer
26      UDR0 = data;}
27   //output string
28   static inline void uart_puts(uint8_t buffer[])
29      {   // send until end of string
30      while (*buffer != 0) {
31          uart_putc(*buffer);
32          buffer++;}}
33   //read character
34   static noinline uint8_t uart_getc(void)
35      {   // wait for character to be received
36      while (!(UCSR0A & (1<<RXC0)));
37      /* return received byte */
38      return UDR0;}
39   //init the hardware uart
40   static inline void init_uart(void)
41      {   // set baud rate for 115,200 using F_CPU =14745600
42      UBRR0H = 0;
43      UBRR0L = 7;     // page 202 set 115,200 baud
44      UCSR0B = (1<<RXEN0)|(1<<TXEN0);//enable Rec & Trans,pages 196-197
45      UCSR0C = (1<<UCSZ01)|(1<<UCSZ00);} //page 197-1984 set for 8 bit
46

line: 7 / 205    col: 26    sel: 0    INS    TAB    mode: Win (CRLF)    encoding: U...
```

Note on line 7 the '|' mark is just showing where the cursor was positioned, please ignore.

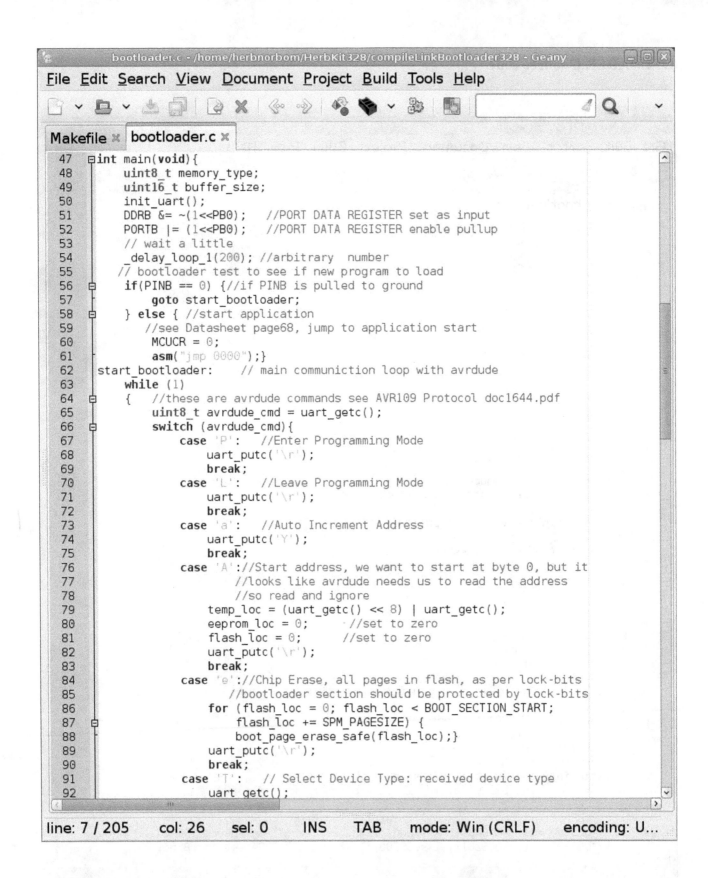

```
47  int main(void){
48      uint8_t memory_type;
49      uint16_t buffer_size;
50      init_uart();
51      DDRB &= ~(1<<PB0);   //PORT DATA REGISTER set as input
52      PORTB |= (1<<PB0);   //PORT DATA REGISTER enable pullup
53      // wait a little
54      _delay_loop_1(200); //arbitrary  number
55      // bootloader test to see if new program to load
56      if(PINB == 0) {//if PINB is pulled to ground
57          goto start_bootloader;
58      } else { //start application
59          //see Datasheet page68, jump to application start
60          MCUCR = 0;
61          asm("jmp 0000");}
62  start_bootloader:    // main communiction loop with avrdude
63      while (1)
64      {   //these are avrdude commands see AVR109 Protocol doc1644.pdf
65          uint8_t avrdude_cmd = uart_getc();
66          switch (avrdude_cmd){
67              case 'P':   //Enter Programming Mode
68                  uart_putc('\r');
69                  break;
70              case 'L':   //Leave Programming Mode
71                  uart_putc('\r');
72                  break;
73              case 'a':   //Auto Increment Address
74                  uart_putc('Y');
75                  break;
76              case 'A'://Start address, we want to start at byte 0, but it
77                      //looks like avrdude needs us to read the address
78                      //so read and ignore
79                  temp_loc = (uart_getc() << 8) | uart_getc();
80                  eeprom_loc = 0;     //set to zero
81                  flash_loc = 0;      //set to zero
82                  uart_putc('\r');
83                  break;
84              case 'e'://Chip Erase, all pages in flash, as per lock-bits
85                      //bootloader section should be protected by lock-bits
86                  for (flash_loc = 0; flash_loc < BOOT_SECTION_START;
87                      flash_loc += SPM_PAGESIZE) {
88                      boot_page_erase_safe(flash_loc);}
89                  uart_putc('\r');
90                  break;
91              case 'T':   // Select Device Type: received device type
92                  uart_getc();
```

line: 7 / 205   col: 26   sel: 0   INS   TAB   mode: Win (CRLF)   encoding: U...

```
 93                    uart_putc('\r');
 94                    break;
 95                case 's'://Read Signature Bytes: send signature bytes for MCU
 96                    uart_putc(SIGNATURE_2);//iom328p.h Datasheet page298 27.3
 97                    uart_putc(SIGNATURE_1);
 98                    uart_putc(SIGNATURE_0);
 99                    break;
100                case 't':// Return Supported Device Codes, term with nullbyte
101                    uart_putc(_AVR910_DEVCODE);
102                    uart_putc(0);
103                    break;
104                case 'S':    // Return Software Identifier, send s[7]
105                    uart_puts((uint8_t *)"RyMax");
106                case 'p':    // Return Programmer Type, 'S' for serial
107                    uart_putc('S');
108                    break;
109                case 'E':    // Exit Bootloader
110                    uart_putc('\r');
111                    break;
112                case 'b'://Check Block Support:
113                    uart_putc('Y');                //return yes
114                    uart_putc(0);                  //another byte
115                    uart_putc(SPM_PAGESIZE);       //block size
116                    break;
117                case 'B'://Start Block Flash Load, read buffer size (in bytes)
118                    buffer_size = (uart_getc() << 8) | uart_getc();
119                    // check buffer size not exceeded
120                    if (buffer_size > SPM_PAGESIZE) {
121                        uart_putc('?');
122                        break;}
123                    //read flash ('F') or eeprom ('E') memory type
124                    memory_type = uart_getc();
125                    if (memory_type == 'F'){
126                        uint16_t i;
127                        uint16_t temp_word_buffer;
128                            if (flash_loc > BOOT_SECTION_START) {
129                                uart_putc(0);}
130                        uint16_t temp_address = flash_loc;
131                        boot_spm_busy_wait();
132                        // read data, wordwise, low byte first
133                        for (i = 0; i < buffer_size/2; i++) {
134                            // get data word
135                            temp_word_buffer = uart_getc() | (uart_getc() << 8);
136                            // write data to temporary buffer
137                            boot_page_fill(temp_address, temp_word_buffer);
138                            // increment by two, since temp address is a byte
```

line: 7 / 205   col: 26   sel: 0   INS   TAB   mode: Win (CRLF)   encoding: U...

File Edit Search View Document Project Build Tools Help

Makefile ×   bootloader.c ×

```
139                        // address, but we are writing words!
140                           temp_address += 2;}
141                    // after filling the temp buffer, write the page
142                    boot_page_write_safe(flash_loc);
143                    boot_spm_busy_wait();
144                    // re-enable application flash section for read
145                    boot_rww_enable();
146                    // store next page's address,as auto-address-increment
147                    flash_loc = temp_address;
148                    uart_putc('\r');
149                }
150          else if (memory_type == 'E'){
151              uint8_t temp_data;
152              uint16_t i;
153              for (i = 0; i < buffer_size; i++) {
154                  temp_data = uart_getc();
155                  eeprom_write_byte( (uint8_t *)eeprom_loc, temp_data);
156                     eeprom_loc++;}
157              uart_putc('\r');
158              }
159              else {uart_putc('?');}
160              break;
161          case 'g':   // Start Block Flash Read, read byte counter
162              buffer_size = (uart_getc() << 8) | uart_getc();
163              // then, read memory type
164              memory_type = uart_getc();
165              // memory type is flash
166              if (memory_type == 'F')
167                  {   // read buffer_size words
168                  uint16_t i;
169                  for (i = 0; i < buffer_size; i += 2) {
170                      uint16_t temp_word_buffer;//define 16bit for word
171                      // read word
172                      temp_word_buffer = pgm_read_word(flash_loc);
173                      // send data as word
174                      uart_putc(temp_word_buffer);         //low byte
175                      uart_putc(temp_word_buffer>>8);      //high byte
176                      // increment address by 2, since a byte address
177                      flash_loc += 2;
178              }}
179              // if memory type is eeprom
180              else if (memory_type == 'E'){
181                  uint16_t i;
182                  for (i = 0; i < buffer_size; i += 1) {
183                      uint8_t temp_buffer;
184                      // read and send byte
```

line: 7 / 205   col: 26   sel: 0   INS   TAB   mode: Win (CRLF)   encoding: U...

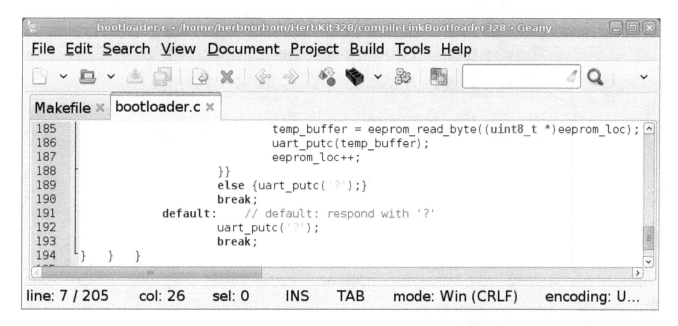

With our error free bootloader.c we are ready to work on our Makefile to load the program on to our microchip. I am going to write this Makefile in a separate directory. I think it is easier to keep everything separate. Change to the 'uploadBootloader328' directory and open your text editor. We are going to define variables and use sections of the Makefile so we can run various parts of it. As I do not want to copy the hex file we need to load from our 'compileLinkBootloader328' directory we are going to use a variable name that has the path and file name for the hex file we want to load. For the variable names you can of course use what you want, just be consistent. The ones I am using seem to fit the purpose of being somewhat self describing.

Makefile Upload bootloader.hex

Go ahead and key the file into your text editor. The file name will be 'Makefile'. Be sure to save it in the correct directory, uploadBootloader328, so you don't erase the other Makefile. We are going to use variable names because there is a lot of repeating going on in this file. For spacing on a new line use TAB and not spaces. Many of the editors handle this automatically to some extent.

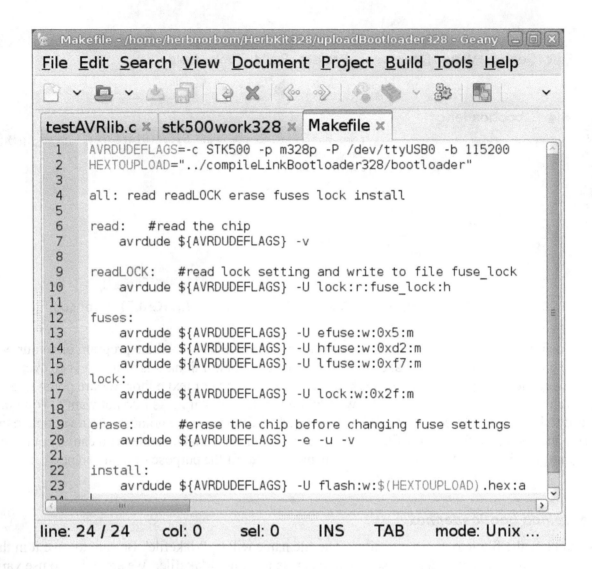

```
1    AVRDUDEFLAGS=-c STK500 -p m328p -P /dev/ttyUSB0 -b 115200
2    HEXTOUPLOAD="../compileLinkBootloader328/bootloader"
3
4    all: read readLOCK erase fuses lock install
5
6    read:   #read the chip
7        avrdude ${AVRDUDEFLAGS} -v
8
9    readLOCK:   #read lock setting and write to file fuse_lock
10       avrdude ${AVRDUDEFLAGS} -U lock:r:fuse_lock:h
11
12   fuses:
13       avrdude ${AVRDUDEFLAGS} -U efuse:w:0x5:m
14       avrdude ${AVRDUDEFLAGS} -U hfuse:w:0xd2:m
15       avrdude ${AVRDUDEFLAGS} -U lfuse:w:0xf7:m
16   lock:
17       avrdude ${AVRDUDEFLAGS} -U lock:w:0x2f:m
18
19   erase:       #erase the chip before changing fuse settings
20       avrdude ${AVRDUDEFLAGS} -e -u -v
21
22   install:
23       avrdude ${AVRDUDEFLAGS} -U flash:w:$(HEXTOUPLOAD).hex:a
```

I suggest you follow the order shown in the following when running the Makefile. Your ATMega328P inserted in the breadboard. Have your STK500 hooked up to the USB port on the computer. You will need the external power to the breadboard 'on'. You will of course be running from the command prompt in our directory where we saved the new Makefile.

- make read   A simple read of your microchip to make sure all is working. This will execute the 'read' section only. Check the fuse hex values.

- make readlock   Read of the lock bits, and writes to file, check the file to make sure okey.

- make fuses   This will set your fuses. If you have them correct you can skip this step.

- make lock   This will set your lock bits. If you have them correct you can skip this step.

- make erase   This will erase the application section of the microchip's flash memory. As long as you have the lock bits set correctly it will not impact the 'BOOT_LOADER_SECTION. You always want to run erase prior to uploading a program.

- make install   This will install our bootloader.hex file on to the microchip.

Once you are feeling pretty good about all the actions taking place you can just type 'make' and all the sections of the Makefile will execute. You of course used a lot of the avrdude commands before when we were working with setting the fuses and lock bits.

BUILD YOUR LIBRARY

We will want to have modules, headers or programs that we can control and easily load into our programs. The Avr library is great, but we really don't want to mess around with it. At least I don't. One program that you can be pretty sure you will use is the UART serial communication. At least our test program will use it and you will get the idea of how to build your own library. Open your text editor and we will create a simple header file. In case you are wondering a header file is just a text file with a '.h' extension. We will create the 'uart.h' file, save it in 'herbClib328'. The complete header is nine lines.

START**

```
#ifndef __UART_H
#define __UART_H

#include <inttypes.h>
#include <stdio.h>

FILE mystream;

void uart_init();

int uart_putchar(char x, FILE *stream);
int uart_getchar(FILE *stream);

#endif
```

END**

Next we want to write the uart.c program. This is very similar to what we wrote in the bootloader.c program.

I am just going to give you a complete program screen shot, as we covered just about all of the items before with the exception of writing to a FILE and *stream. For more information on that check your Datasheet, USART section starting on page 176.

File Edit Search View Document Project Build Tools Help

Makefile × uart.c × uart.h ×

```
1    // uart.c Herb RyMax, Inc. greatly simplied, but just the basics
2    //remember the .h file is just made with an editor
3    // ATmega168 or ATmega328p, 14.7456 MHz clock
4    //page references are to ATmega328 Datasheet
5    #include <stdio.h>
6    #include <stdlib.h>
7    #include <avr/io.h>
8    #include <inttypes.h>
9    #include "uart.h"
10   void uart_init()
11   {
12       UBRR0H = 0;
13       UBRR0L = 7;      //see page 202 set 115,200 baud
14       UCSR0B = (1<<RXEN0) | (1<<TXEN0);  //enable Rec & Trans,page 196
15       UCSR0B |= (1<<RXCIE0); //enable uart RX RECEIVE Interrupt,page196
16       UCSR0C = (1<<UCSZ01) | (1<<UCSZ00); //page 197-198 set for 8 bit
17   }
18   int uart_putchar(char c, FILE *stream) {  //page 195
19       while ((UCSR0A & (1<<UDRE0))==0);   //if UDRE0=1 buffer empty
20                                           //and ready for new data
21           UDR0 = c;      // send keyboard input
22       return 0;
23   }
24   int uart_getchar(FILE *stream) {
25       char x = UDR0; //get data
26       return x;
27   }
28
```

Blur /
or unt

1 file saved.

Now that you have your uart.c program and uart.h header file ready we need to write a Makefile to compile into an output file 'uart.o'.

Enter the following and save as 'Makefile', in the herbClib328 directory.

START**

```
#make file compiling uart.c for herbClib328
all:    uart.o
uart.o: uart.c
        @echo "Starting herbClib compile to build output 'o' file"
        avr-gcc -g -Os -Wall -mmcu=atmega328p -o uart.o -c uart.c
```

END**

After you have the Makefile completed, go ahead and type 'make' from the command prompt in the 'herbClib328' directory.

This will produce the uart.o file. Once you are finished here proceed to the TEST PROGRAM section.

TEST PROGRAM

Now that we have our very own bootloader of course we want to write a program and upload it to our microchip. The purpose of this program is to test our library and see if we have communications with our

PC. We will also define a pin for output and flash a LED. We will use a terminal communication program on the PC, for displaying information from the microchip and simple response back to the microchip from the PC. My examples are going to be shown using PuTTY. Another area that I want to touch on is eeprom memory. This is non-volatile memory that you can store data in. The data is retained when the power goes off. I am just going to write two simple integers to the eeprom, read them back and display them on the console. A little later I will cover reading eeprom using a 'dump' command in avrdude terminal mode.

testAVRlib.c

Complete source code shown using screen shots.

```
//testAVR.c
//simple USART using interrupts and standard avr delay function
//Copyright 2013 HerbNorbom <herb@rymax.biz> 8/30/2013
//Use Putty 115200, data bits 8, parity none,
// stop bit 1
#define F_CPU 14745600
#include <stdio.h>
#include <avr/io.h>
#include <avr/interrupt.h>
#include <avr/pgmspace.h>
#include <inttypes.h>
#include <avr/eeprom.h>
#include <util/delay.h>
#include "../herbClib/uart.h"
void flash_led(){
    PORTC |= (1<<PC5);// turn on LED signal ready and received
    _delay_ms(20);//delay  approx 20 milliseconds LED on
    PORTC &= ~(1<<PC5); // turn off LED
}
ISR(USART_RX_vect)       // interrupt on USART
    {
    flash_led();          //signal data received
    char ReceivedByte;
    ReceivedByte = UDR0;
    printf_P(PSTR("%c"),ReceivedByte);
    if (ReceivedByte =='\r')
        {printf_P(PSTR("\r\n line feed received \r\n"));}
}
```

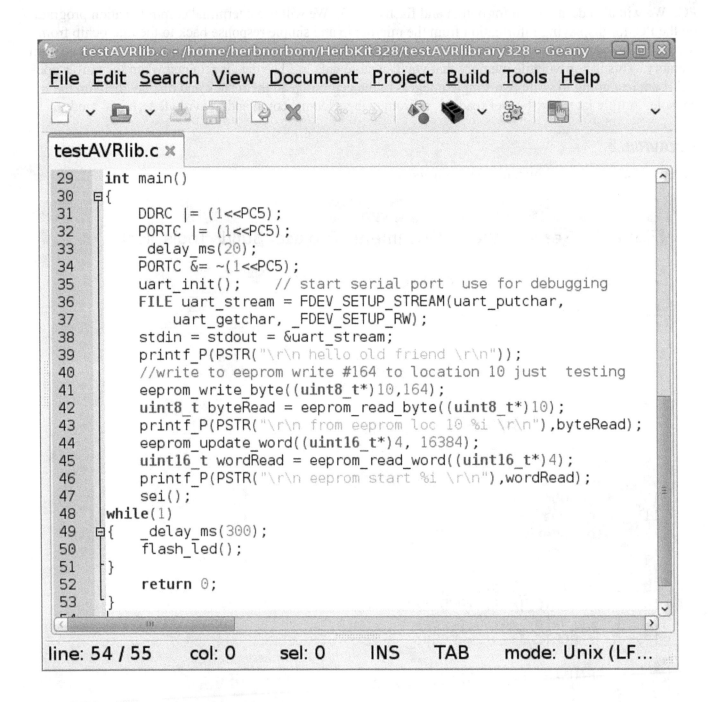

```
29    int main()
30   ⊟{
31        DDRC |= (1<<PC5);
32        PORTC |= (1<<PC5);
33        _delay_ms(20);
34        PORTC &= ~(1<<PC5);
35        uart_init();    // start serial port  use for debugging
36        FILE uart_stream = FDEV_SETUP_STREAM(uart_putchar,
37            uart_getchar, _FDEV_SETUP_RW);
38        stdin = stdout = &uart_stream;
39        printf_P(PSTR("\r\n hello old friend \r\n"));
40        //write to eeprom write #164 to location 10 just  testing
41        eeprom_write_byte((uint8_t*)10,164);
42        uint8_t byteRead = eeprom_read_byte((uint8_t*)10);
43        printf_P(PSTR("\r\n from eeprom loc 10 %i \r\n"),byteRead);
44        eeprom_update_word((uint16_t*)4, 16384);
45        uint16_t wordRead = eeprom_read_word((uint16_t*)4);
46        printf_P(PSTR("\r\n eeprom start %i \r\n"),wordRead);
47        sei();
48    while(1)
49   ⊟{  _delay_ms(300);
50        flash_led();
51    }
52        return 0;
53    }
```

line: 54 / 55   col: 0   sel: 0   INS   TAB   mode: Unix (LF...

Compile Link Assemble Upload testAVRlib.c

With our program written and saved we of course want to compile, link, assemble and upload to our ATMega328P. We will continue using our STK500 ISP. I have had a lot of problems getting the serial programmer PL2303 to work reliably on the Debian-Linux system for the purpose of uploading application programs.

We need one more Makefile. Using your text editor create and save the following with file name Makefile in the same directory as your application program 'testAVRlib.c' in directory '..HerbKit328\testAVRlibrary328'. The complete Makefile is shown in the following along with a number of notes that you should not put in your Makefile.

Makefile	DESCRIPTIONS DO NOT INCLUDE IN Makefile
# program name testAVRlib 9/1/2013 # this is a simple Makefile to compile, link # assemble and upload the testAVRlib.hex file # to the ATMega328p microchip, Herb @ RyMax, Inc	The # means this is a comment line.
LINKFLAGS=-Wl,-u,vfprintf -lprintf_flt	Setup the options needed for linking in variable, easier to handle Linking, Wl (note this is a small letter L, not a '1'). Passing the item after the comma to the linker. What immediately follows the small l or linker command switch is the unique part of the library filename. The '-u' forces the items following to be entered in the output file as undefined. Triggers additional modules from the standand libraries. For outputing values to stream. Part of the c printf family. lprintf_flt allows for floating point. SEE \avr\include\stdio.h approx line 567 for more info.
LINKFLAGS+=-Wl,-u,vfscanf -lscanf_flt	For working with file stream.
LINKFLAGS+=-lm	Suboptions for linker, '-l' (small letter L) means include library name that immediately follows, an 'm' in our case. The 'm' is automatically expanded to the full name of 'libm.a' in our case. The file is located in C:\WinAvr-20100110\avr\lib\avr5 in our case.
LINKOBJECTS=../herbClib328/uart.o	Setup the OBJECTS needed in variable, easier to handle
all: compile assemble upload	Define the sections
compile: testAVRlib.c avr-gcc -g \	Section defined. We are using the avr-gcc compilier, -g for producing debugging information. Note the '\' means the command continued on next line.
-Os \	Optimize for size.
-Wall \	Error warning level set to all
-mmcu=atmega328p \	Specify the ATMEL AVR defined
$(LINKFLAGS) \	LINKER options see above
-o testAVRlib.o testAVRlib.c \	Write outpur to file, here testAVRlib.c output written to testAVRlib.o (Option use small letter o)
$(LINKOBJECTS)	see above
avr-objcopy -j .text -O ihex testAVRlib.o testAVRlib.hex	Copy the testAVRlib.o file to the testAVRlib.hex file and use the library to change to the desired format
assemble: testAVRlib.hex avr-objdump -d testAVRlib.o > testAVRlib.ass	Section defined. Information about the object file, testAVRlib.o is '-d' disassemble and build testAVRlib.ass file
upload: testAVRlib.hex avrdude -c STK500 \	Section defined. Defining our programmer to avrdude using STK500 vs avr109
-p m328p \	the AVR defined device we want to upload to
-P /dev/ttyUSB0 \	USB port our serial programmer is using
-b 115200 \	Baud rate for serial programer
-U flash:w:testAVRlib.hex:a	Memory operation, writing to flash memory our hex file

You may have noticed in the Makefile that when I did a line continue, '\', I put a space before it. Sometimes it appears that it needs the space.

Once you have it completed run it from a prompt in the testAVRlibrary328 directory. For example 'make compile' to test compiling your program. When you are ready type 'make' at the command prompt, and you should see a fairly long display of information. The most important part at the end being that avrdude: verifying number of flash bytes and an avrdude done. Thank you. Of course with no errors showing.

Application Breadboard

You need a separate breadboard. As with our first breadboard I positioned the microchip so that pin 1 is in row 1 of the breadboard. The main difference is the communications, but there are other differences that I will detail.

The USB to TTL Serial Cable from Adafruit PL2303 is used in place of the STK500 on the breadboard. The green wire of the serial cable will connect to PIN2, or the RXD pin. The white wire of the serial cable will connect to PIN3, or the TXD pin. The black wire of the serial cable will connect to the ground. The red wire of the serial cable can be connected to the red rail of the breadboard as it should be putting out 5v via the USB connection. I generally do not connect the red wire and rely on my external power source run through the voltage regulator. The choice is yours, my diagram will show an external power source.

I did not include a resistor on PC6 or PIN1 as we did on the previous breadboard.

As I want a flashing LED I ran a wire from PIN28, PC5 to breadboard row 20. I put a small resistor from row 20 to row 21. Then a small LED from row 21 to blue rail or ground. Remember which way your LED works. The long wire is for + (Anode) and the shorter leg or wire for – (Cathode). The short leg goes into the blue rail. The resistor is to limit current so the LED doesn't blow up or burn out to quickly. There are sites on web to help you do calculations. But do use a resistor.

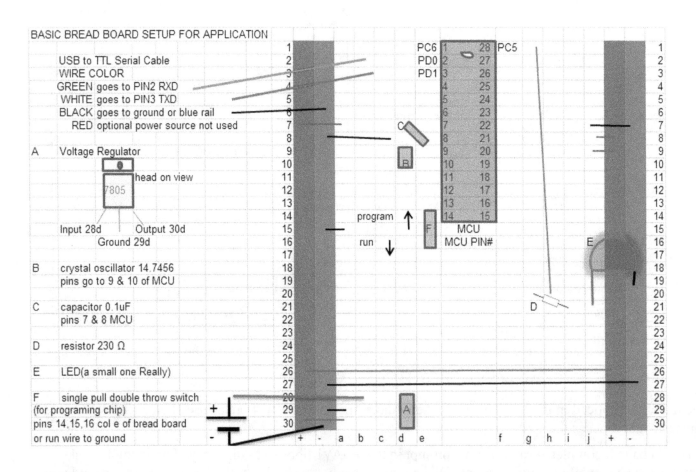

The switch shown as 'F' is not really needed as we are uploading the application program using the STK500 and that breadboard.

Run Your Application Software

Open PuTTY with the following settings, serial, /dev/ttyUSB0, Speed=115200, Data bits =8, Stop bits =1, Parity =None, Flow control = None.   If you have the switch (F in diagram) set it to the 'run' position. Insert the microchip, connect the serial cable to your computer, and turn on the auxiliary power to the breadboard. Turn the auxiliary power back on and you should see the LED flashing and a message displayed on the PuTTY screen similar to the following.

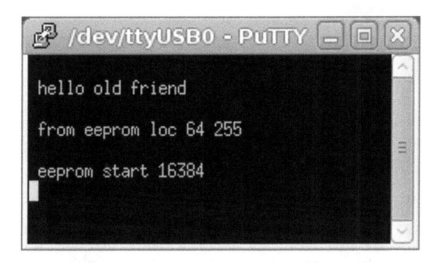

As you can see we have our text message. If you type on the keyboard you should see your input on the PuTTY display, when you press return it should give you the message 'line feed received'. The last topic I want to touch on is reading the eeprom using avrdude in terminal mode.

Avrdude Terminal Mode Read eeprom

I have moved the microchip back to the STK500. With the auxiliary power on, enter the following from the command prompt to enter terminal mode:

 avrdude -c STK500 -p m328p -P /dev/ttyUSB0 -b 115200 -t

Once you are in terminal mode enter the following after the 'avrdude.>' prompt to read a small portion of the eeprom:.

 dump eeprom 0 100

You should get a screen similar to the following.

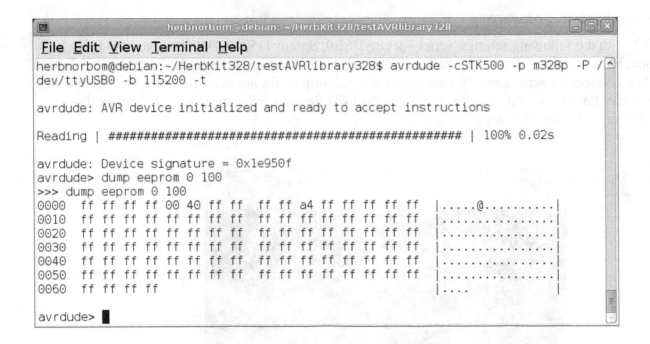

```
                    herbnorbom@debian: ~/HerbKit328/testAVRlibrary328
File  Edit  View  Terminal  Help
herbnorbom@debian:~/HerbKit328/testAVRlibrary328$ avrdude -cSTK500 -p m328p -P /
dev/ttyUSB0 -b 115200 -t

avrdude: AVR device initialized and ready to accept instructions

Reading | ############################################### | 100% 0.02s

avrdude: Device signature = 0x1e950f
avrdude> dump eeprom 0 100
>>> dump eeprom 0 100
0000  ff ff ff ff 00 40 ff ff  ff ff a4 ff ff ff ff ff  |.....@..........|
0010  ff ff ff ff ff ff ff ff  ff ff ff ff ff ff ff ff  |................|
0020  ff ff ff ff ff ff ff ff  ff ff ff ff ff ff ff ff  |................|
0030  ff ff ff ff ff ff ff ff  ff ff ff ff ff ff ff ff  |................|
0040  ff ff ff ff ff ff ff ff  ff ff ff ff ff ff ff ff  |................|
0050  ff ff ff ff ff ff ff ff  ff ff ff ff ff ff ff ff  |................|
0060  ff ff ff ff                                        |....            |

avrdude> █
```

Reading the memory or should I say translating it is not too bad, just remember it is encoded. Back in our application program 'testAVRlib.c' on line 41 we wrote the number 164 to position 10 of eeprom. In the preceding display you can see 'a4' in memory location 10. (The first 'ff' is position 0 when counting). If you convert the 'a4' from hex to decimal you see our number 164. If you look at the right side of the display you see a translation from hex to character. The hex value 40 translates to the character '@'.

Our second write from our program was to memory address 4 and the value was 16384. This is a little more complicated. In memory location 4 we see '00' which tells us the next value (which is also hex) is to be multiplied by 256. First step, the hex value 40 is 64 in decimal. Second step multiply 64 by 256 which gives us 16384. But what if we had but 16385 as input to our program. Here we see that memory location 4 has '01' which means we do as before but add one to the result of 64 * 256. See the following example.

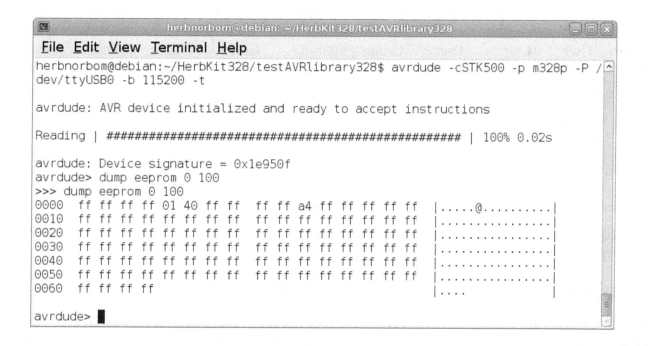

```
herbnorbom@debian: ~/HerbKit328/testAVRlibrary328
File  Edit  View  Terminal  Help
herbnorbom@debian:~/HerbKit328/testAVRlibrary328$ avrdude -cSTK500 -p m328p -P /
dev/ttyUSB0 -b 115200 -t

avrdude: AVR device initialized and ready to accept instructions

Reading | ################################################## | 100% 0.02s

avrdude: Device signature = 0x1e950f
avrdude> dump eeprom 0 100
>>> dump eeprom 0 100
0000  ff ff ff ff 01 40 ff ff  ff ff a4 ff ff ff ff ff  |.....@..........|
0010  ff ff ff ff ff ff ff ff  ff ff ff ff ff ff ff ff  |................|
0020  ff ff ff ff ff ff ff ff  ff ff ff ff ff ff ff ff  |................|
0030  ff ff ff ff ff ff ff ff  ff ff ff ff ff ff ff ff  |................|
0040  ff ff ff ff ff ff ff ff  ff ff ff ff ff ff ff ff  |................|
0050  ff ff ff ff ff ff ff ff  ff ff ff ff ff ff ff ff  |................|
0060  ff ff ff ff                                        |....            |

avrdude> █
```

To exit avrdude terminal mode type 'quit' or ctrl +z. If you have problems with uploading programs to your chip due to "avrdude: verification error; content mismatch" consider that we have set the HFuse to be preserved through a chip erase. You may want to try setting the HFuse hex to da. That is just changing one value, the EESAVE from a 0 to a 1. This will permit erasing of the eeprom memory.

THE END OR THE BEGINNING

I hope that you have learned a lot and had some fun.

Visit the web site www.rymax.biz for additional information. I would like to learn from your experience, you can e-mail me at herb@rymax.biz.

APPENDIX

Linux-Debian Shell Scripts

A few helpful hits first. We are going to be writing non-interactive shells as they behave similar to DOS script files . You can write your script using any text editor, vi or vim, etc. I will be using Geany. This will be a simple file to change to the directory I want to work in. I am going to save the file in my home directory and it will change to the 'HerbKit328' directory and list the directory. (Assuming you have created the directory.)

- The file name doesn't need an extension.

- Comments are a line starting with a pound sign '#'

- You need to have permission to execute or run the script. After you have saved your script open a terminal window and go to the directory where you saved the script. Type ls -l stk500work328 for example. (small letter 'L') The permissions will be shown. Something like the following table, third row.

position 1	2	3	4	5	6	7	8	9	10
directory flag	User read	User write	User execute	Group read	Group write	Group execute	Other read	Other write	Other execute
-	r	w	-	r	-	-	r	-	-
-	r	w	x	r	-	-	r	-	-

After you save the file you need to make it an executable. You can do this from a terminal window be in the directory with your script and type chmod u+x stk500work. Then retype the ls -l stk500work328 and you should see the change as shown on row 4 of the preceding table.

- To run the script from the terminal window, be in the same directory and type. ./stk500work328 or type . stk500work328 (Notice the . and space)

USB0 connections

A couple of comments on using the USB ports with Debian-Linux. First plugging in devices, unplugging them and re-plugging them back in may very well change the USB#. Get used to running the command dmesg and looking at the USB port number assigned. While I recommend you disconnect the USB cord when changing microchip's you may find that using a zif socket to hold the chip provides some degree of safety when inserting and removing the microchip's from the breadboard. A relatively inexpensive zif socket is available from Adafruit, ID 382. Also consider using two USB ports for your devices.

Debian-Linux Commands

Before using understand that many of the commands have options that are not shown here. For those who may have forgotten some simple Linux commands, a very quick refresher course follows. This is only the tip of the iceberg, just listing a few. Before we go any further, a few quick words on commands. They can do damage, they are not very user friendly; they will destroy without asking twice. So make sure the command you enter is the command that you want and that you know what the command is going to do. Remember when you executing a command that involves a filename you may want to generally proceed the filename with a "./". Example "cat ./filename".

cat filname	list contents of file
cat filename > filename2	copy filename to filename2
cd	change to home directory
cd /	change to root directory
cd ..	move up one level in the directory tree
chown newower filename	change the owner of filename to the newowner name
chmod u+x stk500work	example of changing permission of stk500work for the user to execute
clear	clear the screen
cp filename filename2	copy filename to filname2
date	show current day, date and time
df -h	File systems mounted, size, used, avail Use%, where mounted

dmesg	This will show the devices attached, very useful for finding PL2303 and other serial devices attached
echo $SHELL	to see what shell you are running
find -name filename	find the specified filename
id	what user you are and what groups you are in
kill number	If you need to stop a runaway process, number is the process ID (PID)
lp filename	print filename to default printer
lpstat -t	show default printer
lsusb	list usb devices running on computer
lsusb -v	run as sudo for a complete list, with v is a verbose list
mkdir filename	make a new directory
more filename	list the file, will do in pages
mv filename filname2	move or rename filename to filname2
pwd	to see what your current directory is
whoami	to see what yser you are
ps -p$	generates a process error but shows options
ps -T or ps	show all processes on this terminal
ps -A	show all processes running on computer
ps aux	show all process running on computer, user, PID & more
pstree	show all processes in a tree format
ps -p$$	show current PID TTY TIME CMD
uname -a	display version and kernel
rm filename	delete file specified
rmdir directory	remove specified directroy
rm -r directory	remove specified directory and contents of the directory
shutdown -h now	shutdown the computer now, you may need sudo in front of command
who	list all users

Connection Problems

Sometimes we need a clue as to why something is not working. You can look in /var/log/messages, open the file and you can see actions taken.

Bit Manipulation

If you are not familiar with bit manipulation you need to work on understanding this. In the following we will just touch on the subject. Some of the Bitwise Operators are shown in the following table.

Operator	Meaning	Description
&	AND	For combining bytes, both bits must be a 1 to move a 1 to the result. If either bit is a 0 the result will be a 0.
|	OR	For combining bytes, if either bit = 1 then the resulting bit will be a 1.
^	XOR	Bitwise exclusive or. Look at two bytes and compare each bit position. If both bits are a 1 the result is 0. If either bit is a 1 result is a 1. If both bits are 0, result is 0.
>>1	RIGHT SHIFT	Shift all the bits in the byte to the RIGHT and fill vacated bit with a 0.
>>3		Shift all the bits in the byte to the RIGHT 3 positions and fill vacated bits with a 0.
<<1	LEFT SHIFT	Shift all the bits in the byte to the LEFT and fill vacated bit with a 0.
<<3		Shift all the bits in the byte to the LEFT 3 positions and fill vacated bits with a 0.
~	TILDE	Flips every bit in the byte, a 1 becomes a 0 and a 0 becomes a 1.

To clarify some examples, the first table will show the decimal values with corresponding binary value as they are assigned to the byte. In the second table we will perform the operations and show the resulting binary and decimal values. The 'Ref' is like a variable or register name. Also, just to add some additional clarification including the hex values.

REF	DECIMAL	7	6	5	4	3	2	1	0	HEX VALUE
A	0	0	0	0	0	0	0	0	0	0
B	1	0	0	0	0	0	0	0	1	1
C	2	0	0	0	0	0	0	1	0	2
D	3	0	0	0	0	0	0	1	1	3
E	4	0	0	0	0	0	1	0	0	4
F	5	0	0	0	0	0	1	0	1	5
G	6	0	0	0	0	0	1	1	0	6
H	7	0	0	0	0	0	1	1	1	7
I	8	0	0	0	0	1	0	0	0	8
J	9	0	0	0	0	1	0	0	1	9
K	10	0	0	0	0	1	0	1	0	A

Simple examples using the above Reference variables. Where the same Reference variable is referenced go to first table and assume value not changed by the example.

Operations	7	6	5	4	3	2	1	0	DECIMAL VALUE	HEX VALUE
A&B	0	0	0	0	0	0	0	0	0	0
A|B	0	0	0	0	0	0	0	1	1	1
G&H	0	0	0	0	0	1	1	0	6	6

G|H	0	0	0	0	0	1	1	1	7	7
K>>1	0	0	0	0	0	1	0	1	5	5
K<<1	0	0	0	1	0	1	0	0	20	14

PuTTY

For our communications you will need PuTTY© or some other terminal interface program. If you do not have one I suggest you try PuTTY. You can use Synaptic Package Manager, aptitude or apt-get to load PuTTY. You can also go to the main PuTTY Download Page.
http://www.chiark.greenend.org.uk/~sgtatham/putty/download.html. From this page you can select the appropriate file.

Open PuTTY and click on Serial, make appropriate changes. I am setting up for baud of 115200, as this speed is what I plan to use in our test program. Also I have set Flow control to 'None'. The PuTTY help files should have been included if things are not working.

Geany For Linux-Debian

Available under Synaptic Package Manager. Also under aptitude and apt-get install geany.